Loving Israel 101
The Jewish People & God's Promises

Evelyn Hinds

Loving Israel 101

Front Cover Photo by Noam Chen

Courtesy of Israeli Ministry of Tourism

www.goisrael.com

Revised August 16, 2016

Copyright © 2016 Evelyn Hinds

All rights reserved.

ISBN:
ISBN-13: 978-1535565356

i | Page

CONTENTS

Preface

In 2013 the founder of Roaring Lambs Ministry, Garry Kinder, told me he would like to have me do something in support of Israel for the ministry. I began to pray and consider what that might be. Janet Kinder gave me a book to study by Dr. David Reagan, Israel: Rejected or Beloved. Reading that book was the catalyst for the inspiration for a seminar.

Since 2007 I had studied the Messianic writings of Dr. Arnold Fruchtenbaum. What I learned from his writing were a good part of the preparation for Dr. Reagan's book to inspire me to action. Another book that I found helpful in the writing of this manuscript was To the Jew First by Dr. Mal Couch.

I believe God had been leading and teaching me for years to equip me to share what I learned. I designed a post card for advertising and Roaring Lambs promoted the seminar. The response of the church-going people that attended, as well as a few Jewish people, encouraged me to keep at it. This book is written from the seminar material I compiled and my own experiences of learning to love the Jewish people.

Introduction

In the early 1960s I made my first visit to a Jewish Synagogue. Growing up my mother took me and my six brothers and sisters to a church in suburban Kansas City. I attended the youth group when I was in junior high school. One evening in particular made a singular impression on me. Our leader took our group to a synagogue in Kansas City. He wanted us to be familiar with other faiths outside our Christian perspective. For me it was a chance to get out of the house and be with friends so I was happy to go. The minutes we spent in the synagogue stuck in my mind because I remember my internal response. I was surprised that Jews still existed! I thought the bible was like all other stories of history where the peoples and cultures had come and gone. I wasn't one to want to show my ignorance so I'm sure I didn't say much. I doubt that I even uttered that I didn't know any Jews. I would say very few of the other young people had any experience with knowing Jews.

My experience was probably that of a normal teenager in middle America who happened to go to church. As I tell my story of coming to love Israel, I must tell from whence I started. That distance is probably the same as for many others. The church read scriptures with the word Jew in it or Israel but didn't teach about them. I understood the inference that you extracted the principle and applied it to yourself. It was inferred that the church had replaced Israel.

I describe myself as a child of the sixties and therefore, as many others, it followed that I drifted away from church attendance. Deep in my heart I knew that God was in charge and the bible was His word but I didn't have time for it. I was "doing my own thing."

Over the following years, I had fled to church on several occasions seeking answers to my problems and hadn't found much help or answers to my prayers. By 1983, my life was a mess. I sought counseling in and out of the church. I was desperate. I was reading the bible because I knew it must have the answers but my mind was so troubled, I couldn't absorb much. One Sunday, I picked up some leaflets out of the racks at the back of the church. They explained the way of salvation. That was September 15, 1983. I signed my name on a couple of them. I wanted to make sure I got it right with God and would be saved. That night in my bed, in my heart of hearts, I waved the white flag of surrender. "I give up. I don't know how to live this life. You can take my life. If you can do anything with it, it's Yours. I'm going Your way and not my way any longer." I fell asleep knowing I had finally done the most radical thing that I had ever done and I knew it was the right thing! I meant business with God.

I began to notice people smiling at me in the often depressing hospital where I worked. I thought, "They haven't smiled at me before." Then I realized that I, a serious minded young woman with a lot of problems, was smiling at them! I began to have joy. I knew it was God's joy, not mine. I had an excitement building in me that was better than any other excitement. God had heard my prayer! I knew it, I felt it, and I can say that nothing is better than having the Creator of the world pay attention to you.

Not too long after that I watched the movie, The Hiding Place, at my church. The movie told the story of a Christian family in Holland during the Holocaust. I didn't know much about the Holocaust. I learned the Ten Boom family loved the Jewish people and risked their lives to save them. They were arrested and imprisoned. Corrie survived the Concentration Camp but her sister, father, brother, and nephew did not. The real Corrie ten Boom came on at the end of the movie. She was an old woman but I saw peace and joy in her face. I could tell she knew something about living the Christian life that I needed to know.

I want to footnote this experience with a thought. *There is nothing so beautiful as peace and joy in an old face!* Think about it: peace and joy is beautiful in anyone…a baby, a teen, but think about how much more in an old weathered face shining with joy. That person has lived with both joys and sorrows of life and still maintains the joy in their remaining years.

Later I happily discovered that Corrie ten Boom wrote books. Who knew? Books and reading are my thing. I reveled in reading all the Corrie books I could find. She became my mentor. In one book in particular, Each New Day, she told a story, gave a verse, and a prayer for each day. She became like a spiritual grandmother to me through that book. I gobble books but this book slowed me down to one page each day. Through the coming years of going through my problems, I reasoned, "Well, I'm not in a concentration camp, Corrie made it, I can make it."

In 1996 I discovered that I had a particular acting talent to portray old women. I happen to love old women and had ever since I was a child. I loved acting but I had surrendered that along with everything else to God in 1983. But I had the opportunity to help plan a ladies' retreat at my church. I thought, "I love playing an old woman—who will I be, I'll be Corrie ten Boom!" At that first performance, I thought it was my only performance, I delivered lines I heard Corrie speak on a tape. Corrie was telling what her father always answered his friends who warned him of the dangers of being involved in the Dutch underground helping the Jews. "I am too old for prison life but for me it would be an honor to give my life for God's chosen people." Unexpectedly to me, my voiced cracked and I began to weep. My heart was touched by Corrie's father's love for God and for His people. Was that a touch of the anointing on Corrie's life story?

That moment was the beginning of my wake-up call from God regarding who the Jewish people were and their importance to Him. Having had one son myself, I know how a parent feels towards people who don't like their child! I am called to love others but especially God's chosen people.

I couldn't learn enough about Corrie. Through word of mouth I began performing my one woman show as Corrie ten Boom. It quickly became my passion.

Through the years I have interviewed people who knew Corrie, listened to their Corrie stories, collected video and audio recordings of her talks, and read everything I could find about her. As a result, I began to study the Holocaust.

In 2007 a woman made a connection for me with Ruth Wardell, a woman who was somewhat of a legend in Messianic circles. Ruth was in her eighties and lived fairly close to me. After our initial phone conversation, she agreed to come visit me at my home. She drove over to meet me and I was thrilled! From her entrance into my front door and by the time she strode down the hall to the living room, I could tell this was a strong minded woman who meant business. She called herself "Ruth with the Truth!" I thought "Well, I'm Evelyn Ruth with the Truth!" and I knew we could be friends. She immediately became another mentor.

Miss Ruth, as I liked to call her, told me about an introductory Judaic class that she taught at a Messianic synagogue. She even taught some basic Hebrew. I replied that I would attend sometime. I didn't think I would come this semester since the class had already started. She replied in no uncertain terms, "You can quickly catch up." It was clear that not coming now was not an option. I did attend and learned and read about so many things about the Jewish people that I'd never heard of. This class had a "graduation" at the end of it. All the people in the class were required to take part in this graduation. I memorized my part of reciting the blessing over the wine in Hebrew. We all recited our parts before the congregation.

Miss Ruth heard the call of God in 1946 to be a missionary to the Jewish people. She was a single woman and after some schooling she left her home in Canada and went to New York City to begin her work. She worked for the ABMJ, now Chosen People Ministry. She never wavered and never stopped. She never married. She was delightfully one of a kind and also fun-loving. I told her, as I tell others: "Miss Ruth was the most Corrie like woman I've ever known." They were both strong minded, unmarried, focused, and committed until the end. I didn't get to meet Corrie before she passed but God sent Miss Ruth to be part of my journey.

Miss Ruth passed in May, 2014. During the years that I had with her she spoon-fed to me the love of the Jewish people. We spent a lot of time together and became close. I have many great memories but one in particular that illustrates our relationship. We studied the Messianic teaching of her "son in the faith" Dr. Arnold Fruchtenbaum. We were taking a trip to Arnold's Ariel ministry. We were in the car and I was driving us from Dallas to San Antonio to attend a seminar. We were passing through Austin in the late afternoon traffic with the sun in my eyes and she was quizzing me on what I'd learned from the last booklet we'd studied. There was no time to waste with Miss Ruth. You had to be learning something! I had to laugh and kid her about her timing that day. Miss Ruth loved to have fun and we had a great time together as I learned the how and why of loving God's people.

My two inspiring mentors brought me from ignorance to the great blessing of loving God's chosen people! The blessings I've experienced compel me to share what I've learned with others. This book is just the basics as I learned them. If even one reader walks away with a greater love for Israel, I've done my job. I pray that this teaching is the encouragement you need to start you on your path to loving the Jewish people.

Let's begin by seeing who God says the Jewish people are and what He promises to them and those that bless them!

Jews, Gentiles, and Christians

Who are they? Who and what determines it? Let's begin with the Jew. Who is considered Jewish is a much debated topic. There are many opinions out there but it is God's opinion that matters for my purposes. I will quote the scriptures as my authority. So all definitions are "biblically speaking."

Throughout the bible God works through covenants. One of the most important prophecies is found in the Abrahamic Covenant in Genesis 12.

The Lord had said to Abram, "Leave your country, your people and your father's household and go to the land I will show you. I will make you into a great nation and I will bless you; I will make your name great and you will be a blessing. I will bless those who bless you, and whoever curses you I will curse; and all peoples on earth will be blessed through you." (Genesis 12:1-3 NIV)

In a sense the rest of the bible hangs on the Abrahamic Covenant. This covenant is eternal and unconditional. These verses contain a word to the wise--God's unchanging foreign policy to the Gentiles. There are blessings for blessing and curses for cursing.

God promises Abraham a land and a great nation. It was later confirmed through Isaac in Genesis 26: 2-5:

The Lord appeared to Isaac and said, "Do not go down to Egypt; live in the land where I tell you to live. Stay in this land for a while, and I will be with you and will bless you. For to you and your descendants I will give all these lands and will confirm the oath I swore to your father Abraham. I will make your descendants as numerous as the stars in the sky and will give them all these lands, and through your offspring all nations on earth will be blessed, because Abraham obeyed me and did everything I required of him, keeping my commands, my decrees and my instructions." (Genesis 26:2-5 NIV)

It was again reconfirmed through Jacob in Genesis 28:

There above it stood the Lord, and he said: "I am the Lord, the God of your father Abraham and the God of Isaac. I will give you and your descendants the land on which you are lying. Your descendants will be like the dust of the earth, and you will spread out to the west and to the east, to the north and to the south. All peoples on earth will be blessed through you and your offspring. I am with you and will watch over you wherever you go, and I will bring you back to this land. I will not leave you until I have done what I have promised you." (Genesis 28:13-15 NIV)

Gen 32:28 Jacob's name was changed to Israel.

Then the man said, "Your name will no longer be Jacob, but Israel, because you have struggled with God and with humans and have overcome." (Genesis 32:28 NIV)

We can follow these scriptures to define the people of Abraham, Isaac, and Jacob as a nation. That would mean that Jewishness is a nationality. All the people in the world that are not of the nation of Israel are Gentiles. You are either a Jew or you are a Gentile. No one asked for what they are. It was God's decision. Jews did not ask to be God's chosen ones.

The first time the word Jew is used in the bible is in Esther:

Now there was in the citadel of Susa a Jew of the tribe of Benjamin, named Mordecai son of Jair, the son of Shimei, the son of Kish (Esther 2:5 NIV)

The word Jew was said to be derived from the root Judah, which meant praise. It was a name to be proud of.

It follows that one is born either a Jew or a Gentile. Jewishness is a nationality as God has promised. Abraham practiced his faith in God.

So also Abraham *"believed God, and it was credited to him as righteousness."* (Galatians 3:6 NIV)

Judaism is the religion of the Jews. Practicing Judaism doesn't make a Gentile a Jew. It makes him a proselyte.

"The term Israel is never used of Gentiles, whether they are believers or not, nor is it used of the Church; it is used only of Jews." There are two Israels: "Israel the whole composed of all Jews; and Israel the elect, composed of all believing Jews, which is the 'true Israel of God.' " (Fruchtenbaum, *Jews, Gentiles, Christians*, page 20)

Who are the Christians?

Christ was born in Bethlehem and went to Jerusalem. He taught that He was the Jewish Messiah. All the people who responded to the Gospel preached by Jesus' Jewish disciples were Jewish. In Peter's sermon in Acts, the first Church numbered 3,000. (Reagan, *The Jewish People*, page 169)

If we acknowledge our sins and are repentant, the Gospel is simply:

- Christ died for our sins.
- He was buried.
- He rose again on the third day.

This is found in I Cor. 15: 1-4. Believing those things is what constitutes the authentic Christian.

I like the way Eugene Peterson in The Message Bible expresses who are the outsiders and who are the insiders. Gentiles are the outsiders and the Jews are the insiders.

Eph. 2 MSG

Now because of Christ—dying that death, shedding that blood—you who were once out of it altogether are in on everything.

The Messiah has made things up between us so that we're now together on this both non-Jewish outsiders and Jewish insiders. He tore down the wall we used to keep each other at a distance. He repealed the law code that had become so clogged with fine print and footnotes that it hindered more than it helped. Then he started over. Instead of continuing with two groups of people separated by centuries of animosity and suspicion, he created a new kind of human being, a fresh start for everybody.

You're no longer wandering exiles. This kingdom of faith is now your home country. You're no longer strangers or outsiders. You belong here, with as much right to the name Christian as anyone.

Eph. 3

The mystery is that people who have never heard of God and those who have heard of him all their lives (what I've been calling outsiders and insiders) stand on the same ground before God. They get the same offer, same help, same promises in Christ Jesus. The Message is accessible and welcoming to everyone, across the board.

The bible describes the symbol of the Jews being the natural olive tree and Gentiles as branches grafted in.

If some of the branches have been broken off, and you, though a wild olive shoot, have been grafted in among the others and now share in the nourishing sap from the olive root, do not consider yourself to be superior to those other branches. If you do, consider this: You do not support the root, but the root supports you. You will say then, "Branches were broken off so that I could be grafted in." Granted. But they were broken off because of unbelief, and you stand by faith. Do not be arrogant, but tremble. For if God did not spare the natural branches, he will not spare you either. Consider therefore the kindness and sternness of God: sternness to those who fell, but kindness to you, provided that you continue in his kindness. Otherwise, you also will be cut off. And if they do not persist in unbelief, they will be grafted in, for God is able to graft them in again. After all, if you were cut out of an olive tree that is wild by nature, and contrary to nature were grafted into a cultivated olive tree, how much more readily will these, the natural branches, be grafted into their own olive tree! (Romans 11:17-24 NIV)

Gentile believers are not to be arrogant toward the Jews!

"The term Christian was first applied to Gentile believers at the church in Antioch (Acts 11:26). Prior to that Christianity was referred to as "The Way" (Acts 9:2) and its adherents were called "Nazarenes" (Acts 24:5), and it was considered to be a sect of Judaism." (Reagan, *The Jewish People*, page 171)

"Although the Jews originally viewed them (Messianic Jews) as a sect of Judaism, they were rejected by the Jewish establishment after the Bar Kochba revolt against the Romans (132-135AD)." (Reagan, *The Jewish People*, page 171)

The Messianic Jews went along with the revolt initially but some of the Jews thought Bar Kochba was the Messiah. This was the point that the Jews and the Messianic Jews separated.

In the early years many Gentiles came to faith in Jesus through the preaching of Jesus' Jewish disciples and the witness of other Jewish believers. Tragically, history proves the Gentiles became arrogant towards the Jews. Anti-Semitism grew in the church. The early Church fathers spread hatred and separation from the Jews. From the 4th Century until 1800, this arrogance resulted in Jewish believers virtually disappearing from the Church.

In spite of the horrible failure of the church, from 1800 to today there are increasing numbers of Jewish believers, by the grace of

God! Christians began to wake up to the importance of the Jewish people and our call to witness to the Jews.

Christianity is, as always, a matter of an individual's faith. Salvation in the Old Testament is the same as the New Testament. It is by grace, through faith.

Judaism is the religion of the Jews. Christian believers do not become "spiritual Jews." That may sound nice but it is nonsense. You can't change what you are born! Some people become what is known as "Jewish-want-a-bees." Not only is that an exercise in futility, it is totally not necessary. Look at the promises made to the Gentiles. We have been grafted in!

To clarify, loving Israel means loving Jewish people and their land promised to them by God. The bible also uses Jerusalem to refer to the land and the people.

Pray for the peace of Jerusalem: May those who love you be secure. (Psalm 122:6NIV)

Another term used is Zion and that is the land of Israel. Zionism is love for the land and the Jewish people. Today you might hear of anti-Zionists. That is simply just anti-Semitism, which is a hateful prejudice against Jews.

In light of God's promise to Abraham, how many Jews are there in the world today? When I ask people most frequently I hear, "Oh, there are lots of them." The facts are surprising to me also. There are about fifteen million Jewish people in the world. That makes them .2% of the population. So few people who have given the world so much!

The Jews gave us our Savior yet anti-Semitism grew in the church.

Replacement Theology

I first heard the term replacement theology expressed in a negative tone. Until recently I'd never heard about it to even have an opinion. I'd never seen any church that advertised it. It sounded wrong in light of all I was learning about God's love for His chosen people. However, as I recalled the teaching of different mainline protestant churches I had attended, this theology was inferred. If a scripture says Israel, just substitute yourself in their place. The churches I attended hardly ever mentioned Jews.

I was an English major in college and very familiar with symbolic language. Using Israel as a symbol for Christian believers came very natural to me. Finding the principle and then seeing how it applied to me was the way I read and learned. However, I have learned that works in some passages in the bible but not all. When it says Israel, it means Israel, His chosen ones.

Dr. David Reagan explains the concept of Replacement Theology in his book. The teaching is not new at all. Soon after the Apostles had died, (100-106 A. D.), Justin Martyr taught Church had replaced Israel, within 80-100 years Jews were called "Christ killers." (Reagan, *The Jewish People*, page 172) This began by forbidding the Jews to practice Passover. Evangelism to the Jews virtually stopped and soon the church was all Gentile. So soon after Christ died, the outsiders had edged out the insiders!

Reagan, Anti-Semitism article from the Lamplighter (Oct. 2007):

"...for almost 2,000 years the Church at large, both Catholic and Protestant, has maintained that due to the fact the Jews rejected Jesus as their Messiah, God poured out His wrath on them in 70 A. D., destroying their nation and their temple, and that He has washed His hands of them, leaving them with no purpose whatsoever as a nation. In short, because of their rebellion against God in their rejection of Jesus, God has replaced Israel with the Church, transferring the blessings promised to Israel to the Church. This is called "Replacement Theology," and those who believe in it constitute the majority of professing Christians today."

Scripture explains that Israel is the olive tree and Gentile believers have been grafted in. We have in no way replaced the Jews. We are not and never will be Jews. We are not to be prideful or boasting towards Israel. We have not edged out His chosen people!

Replacement Theology is clearly unscriptural. God speaks in Leviticus that He will not break His covenant with them.

Yet in spite of this, when they are in the land of their enemies, I will not reject them or abhor them so as to destroy them completely, breaking my covenant with them. I am the Lord their God. But for their sake I will remember the covenant with their ancestors whom I brought out of Egypt in the sight of the nations to be their God. I am the Lord.' " (Leviticus 26:44-45 NIV)

We can refer back to the Abrahamic Covenant to read God's eternal and unchanging foreign policy for the Gentiles. "I will bless those that bless you and I will curse those that curse you." That is an eternal promise. A prideful attitude towards the Jews is a curse.

Replacement Theology is a form of anti-Semitism. It is a curse to the Jews. Remember that God will curse those that curse His people. This theology eliminates witnessing to the Jews. It grieves me that this theology is so prevalent in the churches. Jews must be told the truth that there is only one way for them to be saved.

Jesus answered, "I am the way and the truth and the life. No one comes to the Father except through me. (John 14:6 NIV)

I pray that Christians will wake up to our responsibility to tell the Jews that we worship their Messiah and how He has changed our lives. God has not rejected His people!

Satanic forces have infiltrated our churches and perverted the truth. The history of the Jews will bear this out.

History of the Jews

Volumes have been written on the history of the Jews but for our purposes we need just a simple overview. There is one book that explains Jewish history and faith found in the bible in an easy to understand way, Christianity is Jewish. It came to be written after Edith Schaeffer was asked by a Jewish family to explain why she was so much nicer to them than other Gentiles. She explained her faith that came from the Jewish faith and history found in the bible. She explained that there are two lines in the bible regarding beliefs:

Faith: Abel, Noah, Abraham, Moses, Isaiah, John, Christ, Peter, Paul

Unbelief: Cain, Works, False Worship, Golden Calf, Baal

I like to call the line of faith, God's way. Unbelief is in the line of Cain and is human being's rebellious nature, "I have a better idea!"

Schaeffer's two lines are a quick overview of the bible. I explained this recently to a friend and she said, "Why have I never heard of this before?" Indeed! We often make things complicated when the simple overview might serve us better.

Schaeffer carefully explained the obvious but generally unknown fact that Christianity is Jewish! Jesus is the promised Jewish Messiah. The sacrifice for sin started with Abel and a lamb. Christ came to be the sacrificial lamb for all who believed.

Then one of the elders said to me, "Do not weep! See, the Lion of the tribe of Judah, the Root of David, has triumphed. He is able to open the scroll and its seven seals." (Revelation 5:5 NIV)

That person is Christ, the Jewish Messiah, both our Lamb and Lion.

My mentor, Miss Ruth, shared with me another simple overview of history. It was about 2,000 years from Creation to Abraham and about 2,000 years to Christ and another 2,000 years to today.

Creation (2,000 years)→ Abraham (2,000 years)→ Christ (2,000 years)→today

Another tool Miss Ruth shared with me was a chart of a general time line of the bible. She used it to teach Jewish children their history. Hers was complete with pictures but I have given the text below. I have found it helpful in studying the bible.

2,000 years to the time of Abraham Covenant: Genesis 12:1-3 Unconditional, Everlasting

Isaac→Jacob→Joseph 400 years in Egypt

Moses→ Exodus (Nation Promise)→Land, Joshua conquer (Land Promise)

Time of the Judges→United Kingdom under Saul, David

Solomon (Temple built)

Divided Kingdom: Israel, Fall Samaria→Assyrian Captivity

Judah, Fall to Babylon→Babylonian Captivity

Return to Jerusalem: Time of the Prophets, rebuilding the Temple, Wall

400 years of silence

John the Baptist, Jesus (Seed Promise)

2,000 years of the Church Age

The Church Age time line for the Jews is simplified below:

70 AD fall of Jerusalem→Jews Dispersed

Sins of church fathers: Chrysostom (347-407)→Crusades→Luther →

Lies circulated about Jews, Political church

Hitler, Nazis following Luther

Pogroms, Dispersion, Camps, Annihilation→

Out of the ashes of the Holocaust→return to the land, reviving the language→Modern day Israel

The establishment of Israel as a state after the dispersion that had lasted nearly 2,000 years is a miracle that only God could have done! It is unprecedented.

All the factors involved had been coming together in God's timetable for years. In the 1800's Jews started to trickle back to Israel. In 1840 God had awakened an English theologian named Darby to the evil of replacement theology and he began to awaken the church to the promises to the Jewish people. He began to visit the land of Palestine.

From Lithuania, a Jew, Eliezer Ben Yehuda, (1858-1922) immigrated to Palestine with a mission to revive the Hebrew language. It was almost to the point of being extinct because so few Jews spoke it. Today Hebrew is spoken in Israel! Dr. Fruchtenbaum says Hebrew is the language of heaven!

In 1896, a Hungarian Jew Theodor Herzl (1860-1904) became

obsessed with the idea of a Jewish state after he experienced French anti-Semitism. This followed the infamous Dreyfus Affair. Herzl wrote a book calling for a Jewish state. Zionism began to grow. He didn't live to see the Jewish state but some say he is the father of Israel.

World War I and the British conquests allowed Britain's Lord Balfour to open up Palestine for immigration in 1917. This was the land promised to Israel. Prophetically this Balfour Declaration was one of the most significant declarations of the century.

In the 1920's there was a surge in Zionism. Jews had a desire to live in the homeland. They began to immigrate from all over the world. Kibbutz were formed for the people to live and work the land. Golda Meir and her husband immigrated at this time. The movie, Golda, is a wonderful history of the making of Israel. It is the amazing story of one of the future Prime Ministers of Israel beautifully portrayed by Ingrid Bergman. Golda's writings are also available through the internet and are a delight to read. She was a brilliant woman and wrote just like she talked. She was a strong and single-minded woman focused on the Jewish state.

In 1947 the United Nations voted to allow Israel to be born. May 14, 1948 David Ben-Gurion signed the declaration of independence.

Can a country be born in a day or a nation be brought forth in a moment? (Isaiah 66:8 NIV)

Yes!

I heard Dr. David Hocking say that he remembers gathering around the radio with his Jewish father on that day. He reported they didn't know what the nation would be called until it was revealed that day. The land would be called Israel. The Jews finally had some of the land promised to them. Israel was a state! President Truman immediately signed the document that recognized Israel. America has been blessed for that!

Israel was then attacked by five neighboring countries but it miraculously survived. In the 1967 war the brave Jewish soldiers finally won sovereignty in Jerusalem. Until then they were banned from East Jerusalem and the Temple Mount.

The Jews have been a persecuted people throughout their history but they continue to survive. How? Without the help of the God of Israel there is no answer.

In "Concerning the Jews," Mark Twain wrote:

> "He could be vain of himself, and be excused for it. The Egyptian, the Babylonian, and the Persian rose, filled the planet with sound and splendor, then faded to dream stuff and passed away; the Greek and the Roman followed, and made a vast noise, and they are gone; other peoples have sprung up and held their torch high for a time, but it burned out, and they sit in twilight, or have vanished. The Jew saw them all, beat them all, and is now what he always was, exhibiting no decadence, no infirmities of age, no weakening of his parts, no slowing of his energies, no dulling of his alert and aggressive mind. All things are mortal but the Jew; all other forces pass, but he remains. What is the secret of his immortality?"

The answer to the survival of the Jewish people is rooted in the Abrahamic Covenant. It is an eternal and unconditional covenant.

The prophet Jeremiah prophesied Israel's survival.

This is what the Lord says, he who appoints the sun to shine by day, who decrees the moon and stars to shine by night, who stirs up the sea so that its waves roar-- the Lord Almighty is his name: Only if these decrees vanish from my sight, declares the Lord , will the descendants of Israel ever cease to be nation before me.”

This is what the Lord says: “Only if the heavens above can be measured and the foundations of the earth below be searched out will I reject all the descendants of Israel because of all they have done,” declares the Lord. (Jer. 31: 35-37 NIV)

Praise God! This is the God we serve! He is a covenant making and covenant keeping God. Even so Satanic forces are still at work.

Destroy the Jews

Can the Jews be destroyed? Let's look at what the bible says.

Yet in spite of this, when they are in the land of their enemies, I will not reject them or abhor them so as to destroy them completely, breaking my covenant with them. I am the Lord their God. But for their sake I will remember the covenant with their ancestors whom I brought out of Egypt in the sight of the nations to be their God. I am the Lord.' " (Leviticus 26:44-45 NIV

The promise from Genesis 17:7:

I will establish my covenant as an everlasting covenant between me and you and your descendants after you for the generations to come, to be your God and the God of your descendants after you. (Genesis 17:7 NIV)

These two passages make it clear that the covenant with Abraham is eternal. This has been playing out historically through the centuries. The Jews have had great persecution, many enemies, and many attempts to wipe them off the face of the earth. However, God's word has remained true and the Jewish people still remain.

One biblical account of such hatred is found in the book of Esther. Esther was married to the king. Her uncle was Mordecai, the Jew. There was an evil man who hated Mordecai and the Jews. He built a gallows to hang Mordecai. Because of Esther's daring access to the king, the plot was exposed and the evil Haman was hanged on the gallows instead.

Christians are so eager to claim the blessings promised in the bible to Jews but what about the curses promised to them? This is something we need to consider when reading our bible. The curses and blessings go together. As much as we consider the blessings promised us for blessing the Jewish people, there are curses for cursing. There is a principle that occurs in scripture that curse for curse in kind will result. It is illustrated completely by the story of Esther. (Fruchtenbaum, *How to Destroy the Jews*, page 6)

Failing to witness to the Jews is a form of cursing or boasting against them. There is a curse promised.

Winston Churchill made this observation about the Jews:

> "Some people like the Jews, and some do not. But no thoughtful man can deny the fact that they are beyond any question, the most formidable and the most remarkable race which has appeared in the world." (Reagan, *The Jewish People*, page 21)

Still, anti-Semitism still thrives if we look at our history.

History of Anti-Semitism

Satanic forces work to attempt to stop the fulfillment of God's plans. The first promise of Jesus (seed of woman) is in Gen. 3:15. Satan was promised His ultimate fate. That began his war with God and anyone or anything to do with God. It continues today. He hates everything God loves and he hates God's plans. He wants to kill the Jewish people so that God cannot fulfill His plan.

Anti-Semitism infiltrated the church in the early days. The Gentile believers became arrogant towards the Jews. Church became part of the government. The political church fathers perpetuated the anti-Semitism. The teaching of replacement theology had its roots in anti-Semitism and the Jews were not witnessed to. Persecution and isolation of Jews became part of the political church's agenda.

Beginning with the First Crusade in the eleventh century, Jewish villages were destroyed. Martin Luther began his ministry with a love for the Jews but by his old age wrote, "If it is a mark of a good Christian to hate the Jews, what excellent Christians all of us are." The Jews became the scapegoat for all problems. The bubonic plague, AD 1348-49, was blamed on the Jews. They were marginalized, then isolated in communities, ghettos. Jews were even forced to convert to the political church religion! This religion has nothing to do with the true faith that Jesus proclaimed.

Jesus gives everyone a choice!

Spain, labeled their Jews, the Marranos, meaning pigs. In 1492 Jews were driven out of the country. Columbus sailed that same year of the expulsion from Spain. He took a number of Jews as part of his crew and some have speculated that Columbus was Jewish.

A false prophet, Zevi, proclaimed himself Messiah in 1648. He eventually converted to Islam and brought great disillusionment to the Jews and many ceased to believe there would ever be a Messiah. Hitler claimed to be following Luther. Jews were called Christ killers. German people were told that the Jews had to be wiped out. (Mal Couch, *To the Jew First*, pages 38-45)

Hitler started with isolation and persecution of the Jews that built over the years and ended with the "Final Solution." Mass extermination! Jews saw the crosses on their Nazi killers and feared anything to do with Christianity.

The Church has blood on its hands. Our history is shameful. Jews have been wrongfully called Christ killers. Why did Christ have to die? For my sins, for your sins. Christ himself said of his life:

No one takes it from me, but I lay it down of my own accord. (John 10:18 NIV)

Satan is alive and well and perpetuates the anti-Semitism. Recently, there was a French journalist in the news. He filmed himself being persecuted as he walked a street in France. Anti-Semitism is again on the rise there. Since then there have been deadly terrorist attacks. Just read the news, it's everywhere.

One of the best explanations I have found of the problem between Israel and its Arab neighbors has been done on a five minute video by Dennis Prager.

Prager Video: Middle East conflict made simple.
www.youtube.com/watch?v=8EDW88CBo-8

Simply, if the Arabs would put their guns down to live in peace, there would be peace. If Israel put their guns down, Israel would be wiped off the map.

In the early days of becoming aware of the importance of the Jews I wondered why the Jews are so universally persecuted. The more I study and learn about the Jews and look around me, the more I see the hideous work of Satan. It is not explainable. It permeates the world we live in and we need to be alert to Satan's sometimes subtle ploys. Look for anti-Semitism and you will find it.

Let's consider one horrific, unthinkable act of anti-Semitism in the 20th Century.

The Holocaust

Anti-Semitism is as old as Satan but World War II and the rise of Adolf Hitler worked the single most destructive act of the Holocaust.

I began to study the Holocaust as a result of studying Corrie ten Boom's life. Over the years through Corrie's writings and talks I learned more about her family's connection with the Jews. Corrie tells the story that her father told her. In 1844, a pastor asked her grandfather to start a prayer group for the Jewish people. Corrie said, "He'd never thought of it but he began to invite his friends and they prayed." Corrie explained that from that came a love for the Jewish people that was passed down through the grandfather. When she was a child she said a painting of a famous Dutch Jew who was a believer hung in their home. Her father also made many friends among the Jews and enjoyed conversation with them about biblical subjects. He loved discussions with the Rabbis.

Corrie reported that her older brother became interested in studying Hebrew and eventually became what she called "like a pastor" to the Jewish people. She wrote that as early as 1925 her brother, Willem, began to warn the family of the danger that the Jewish people were in in Germany. Hostility and violence against the Jews had emerged. Father ten Boom said, "I pity the Germans that they have dared to touch the apple of God's eye!"

The Nazi's invaded Holland in 1940 and the Ten Booms began to be part of the Dutch underground group helping to hide the Jews. In 1944, one hundred years after Grandfather started a prayer group for the Jewish people, Corrie's own family was arrested in that very same home where the prayer group began. Corrie called that "A divine but not to be understood answer to prayer." Indeed! I am reminded that God's ways are not our ways.

Through my study I also became interested in Jewish survival stories. When I met Miss Ruth, she furnished me with several books about Jewish survivors. On a trip to Canada, in a museum shop I found tapes of survivors telling their stories. Precious resources! I continue to collect books and recordings.

Along with my study, I became interested in traveling to Israel. I felt sure I would go sometime but didn't know how, when. In 2006 I was invited to be a guest on a radio program and I suggested that they might like to air it on Yom HaShoah, Israel's Holocaust Memorial day. I went to the internet to do a little research before that and I learned that the next year, in 2007, the holiday fell on Corrie's birthday. Corrie's birthday was a significant day for several reasons. She died on her birthday and her memorial tree at Israel's Holocaust Museum was struck by lightning one year and that occurred on her birthday. I believed 2007 was the time to make the trip! I prayed and God provided a wonderful group from Georgia that was traveling there and would be in Jerusalem during that April 15 timeframe.

Through an acquaintance, I learned about a Christian connected with the Holocaust Museum in Jerusalem. I emailed his contact at Yad Vashem. As a result, my husband and I were given tickets to the evening ceremony honoring the Holocaust victims. On that evening we left our group at the hotel and got a taxi to the museum. All entrants had to go through security. Never have we been subject to such security screening, including an interview about why we were there. The place was overflowing with people from all over the world. There were Jewish people, foreign dignitaries, Israeli military, and Gentiles like us honored by being included in the evening. The service was in Hebrew which we couldn't understand but we felt it. I'll never forget the atmosphere of that Spring evening in Jerusalem. It was Holy.

The next day we joined our tour group for a visit back to Yad Vashem. I was aware that the museum also honored the Righteous Gentiles who helped them during the Holocaust. Corrie was invited and planted her memorial tree there in 1968. She wrote that she felt the somber sadness of the place.

The day we were there the museum was again filled with people, including many Israeli school groups and tourists. Since it was the Yom HaShoah holiday, the ban on use of cameras was lifted. Rob and I walked through the exhibits, reading as much as we could, seeing the photos and also hearing the stories being played on video screens. One particular TV screen stopped me. It was a Jewish woman from Holland that was telling her story. English subtitles were at the bottom of the screen. I thought I saw Ten Boom house at the bottom. I told Rob to get his camera and we watched again. The woman told her story that as a child, her mother felt that they would be captured and hid her and her sister in the closet. When the Gestapo came her mother came to the closet to get her coat. She quietly told them to go to the Ten Boom house. They evidently did that and survived but reported that they never saw their mother again.

The museum is in many ways a sensory overload. Overwhelming sadness. I felt overwhelmed but Rob was able to get the photo of the screen with the name Ten Boom on it and I count that as one of my God-incidences, a hug from God. I knew He had orchestrated that experience and He was with us.

Outside the museum building there is an avenue and courtyard of the Righteous Gentiles. Beautiful trees are planted there and I knew we would see Corrie's tree. We had been sitting in that courtyard the night before and we were near her tree but I didn't realize it.

I had heard from several sources that one year that there was a thunderstorm in Jerusalem and one tree was struck by lightning and it died. It was Corrie's tree and that happened on her birthday. Her tree was replanted and the guides like to take tourists there and tell the story. We got a photo there as well. Her tree is growing but not as tall as many of the others.

Let's remember the facts of the Holocaust. Six million Jews perished. Between 1933-1945 the European countries lost up to 90% of their Jewish population. The highest numbers were lost in Poland. I think of the Polish Jews that remained and wonder how they coped when nine out of ten people they knew were just gone! Starved, murdered, gassed and burned in the camps.

Consider also that many others perished also. There were Gentiles who risked their life working in the underground groups to help save the Jews. Corrie's family was just one of those. Her father died after being imprisoned, her brother died from illness after returning from prison, her sister died in Ravensbruck camp, and later she learned that her nephew died in Bergen-Belsen.

I learned that in recent years Corrie's father and sister have been added to the list of Righteous Gentiles. Corrie would have been pleased because she wrote that it didn't feel right that she had been singled out to be honored when others in her family deserved the honor as well.

I am continuing to learn more as I search for and study the Jews and the Holocaust. Another trip would help me to take another step in understanding.

A Holocaust Trip

In June, 2015 my husband and I had the opportunity to go on a Holocaust remembrance tour of Germany and Poland with Chosen People ministry. Our group started in New York City as we visited some of the historic sites where the Jewish people lived, many after fleeing the Holocaust. I learned that the Williamsburg bridge from Manhattan to Brooklyn was known as the Jew's highway because of the numbers of Jews that moved into Brooklyn. We also ate at the famous Jewish Katz Deli.

Berlin was our next stop and we had the delight to go to a Messianic Jewish church, Beit Sar Shalom. The pastor is a Jewish believer from Russia. He shared his incredible, and often humorous, testimony. His congregation was overwhelming hospitable to us and served us homemade Yiddish food. The pastor Vladmir Pittman reported that Germany is considered a desirable and safe place for Jews. Reportedly 300,000 have immigrated in the last ten years. Even some Israeli citizens have immigrated.

We were told Germany has done many things to apologize for the Holocaust. Holocaust denying is considered a criminal offense. Germany is blessed now with having Jewish people again.

Touring Berlin we saw Checkpoint Charlie, the remains of the Wall, and government buildings. We went to the childhood home of Dietrich Bonhoeffer. He was one of the too few Christian pastors who fought against the Nazi's plans. He was arrested and died in prison.

Another memorable spot was the historic site where the Nazis planned the "final solution" for the Jewish people, Wanassee. There were exhibits there and documents showing the incredible atrocities that were cold-bloodily planned in that mansion. Included in the exhibits was some surviving artwork done by the prisoners. The prisoners had drawn how the bodies were stacked on top of each other. One piece of artwork was labeled Ravensbruck, 1944. That's when Corrie was there and where her sister died. Corrie was released from that camp on a "clerical error" in December of 1944.

Another art installation in the city is in an outside plaza. is a large monument to the murdered Jews. It is a maze like structure where you enter but are quickly out of sight. The walls are uneven and people seem to disappear. Cleary many of the German people are sorry for what happened in their land.

Berlin also has the remains of a bombed synagogue with exhibits that we were able to see. Einstein was reported to have played his violin there. One photo of the congregants showed the artist Max Liebermann on the front row.

We went to a Holocaust museum. One piece of artwork was at the end of a dark hall with a door to the bright outside, the future. Outside, I cannot get out of my mind how it felt to walk on series of pathways with terribly uneven walkways. Walking through it has the effect of making one nauseous. The intent was described to bring to mind how the Jewish people felt when they were displaced from their homes. Life in exile. Incredible disorientation.

One dark room in the museum had a sliver of light coming in at the top. It reminded of me of Corrie's imprisonment. She described how important just a small patch of light is to a prisoner living in a dark cell.

Jews had a great love for Germany and had been there since the fourth century. The Holocaust was a tragic and murderous response to that love.

We flew from Berlin to Warsaw to tour the Warsaw ghetto. It was used between 1940-45 to imprison Jews. Photos of the infamous time were posted for all to see. We toured a Jewish cemetery that had been desecrated. Senseless hatred towards the Jews. We toured the modern museum of the Holocaust and saw the large outdoor monument to the bravery of the heroes of the Ghetto uprising.

Chosen People has a Messianic congregation in Warsaw and they opened their doors to us. We were told that Jewish people today feel no anti-Semitism in Poland. Again we were offered hospitality.

The pastor was a Jewish man from Poland. His daughter explained how he came to discover that he was Jewish. He was a Christian pastor and went to the hospital with his uncle to visit his dying mother. They took her purse with them when they left. Inside was an old worn postcard of the Jordan river. This pastor asked his uncle, "Why would mother keep this in her purse?" The uncle replied, "Because we are Jews." That was a thunderbolt for the pastor. He had never known because they lived as Gentiles. His daughter explained that when her grandmother was witnessed to by Gentiles and believed in Jesus, they told her never to speak of Jews again and do everything opposite of Jews. At that point this pastor's ministry changed to a Messianic congregation.

We learned that the Jewish people had loved Poland. The word means "rest here." The Jews had lived there for nine centuries. There were three and a half million there before the Holocaust. Today there are about ten thousand.

On our tour of Krakow, we stopped at the museum in the now famous Schindler factory. The downtown square of Krakow has a fenced area of wrought iron menorahs. We had a most memorable dinner near there. We were entertained with Yiddish music sung by Gentiles who have resurrected the musical history and were honoring it.

Auschwitz in Poland stands out as the most incredible witness of what happened to the Jewish people. As I looked at the photographs and into the faces of those getting off the train there, I could see that they were totally unaware that minutes later they would be killed. As I looked at the piles of shoes in the exhibits, I saw ladies' heels that would be very fashionable today. The women had appeared to have worn their best on the journey to their ultimate death.

There were busloads of tourists from all over the world visiting the site of Auschwitz' horrific death camps the cold rainy day we were there.

For centuries eighty percent of the Jews in Poland lived in shtetls, small towns. We took a bus tour of the countryside and toured one village that has a museum in a former Jewish synagogue. You can look it up on the internet, the Chmielnik synagogue. As I stepped on the large stone entrance step I could see how the years of Jewish feet entering there had worn a deep but smooth indentation in that stone. How many years, how many feet did it take to make that considerable wear? Inside we saw film footage of happy days there before the war. Priceless memories. We toured Jewish cemeteries that had been desecrated. My instinct was "This needs to be fixed!" but the damage has been left as a testimony of what occurred. We were told some Polish farmers shamefully used headstones from Jewish graves to pave their barns.

"Why are the Jews so hated???" It doesn't make sense. Again, it is Satanic! The Jews knew they were being persecuted but didn't seem to think they would be killed. Who would have believed that Hitler would have done what he did? Unthinkable! But it happened and history shows us that it could happen again. Christians must stand in solidarity with God's chosen people!

The Jewish people have a slogan: "Never Again!" As Christians we can heartily agree and support the Jewish people against the Satanic forces. We can be watchmen, Isaiah 62:6 says, "I have posted watchmen on your walls, O Jerusalem."

A comment from the news in 2015 agrees and makes the point, we need to mean it.

"The rise of European anti-Semitism is, in reality, just a return to the norm…On the 70th anniversary of Auschwitz, mourning dead Jews is easy. And, forgive me, cheap. Want to truly honor the dead? Show solidarity with the living—Israel and its 6 million Jews. Make "never again" more than an empty phrase. It took Nazi Germany seven years to kill 6 million Jews. It would take nuclear Iran one day." (www.aish.com/jw/s/Do-We-Really-Mean-Never-Again.html

Anti-Semitism will not go away. There is another dangerous theology that has infiltrated our churches.

Dual Covenant Theology

I heard my believing Jewish friends express a special abhorrence for preachers who don't believe or practice witnessing to the Jews. One said, "They'll witness to an atheist, a Moslem, but not a Jew, my relatives!" It seems peculiar reasoning to me also.

In my journey learning about the Jewish people, I had not heard of this theology practiced in Christian churches until I began reading David Reagan's books. He explains that Dual Covenant theology is not a new concept. It began in the 12th Century. The theology is that Jews are saved through Mosaic Covenant and Gentiles are saved through the New Covenant. That may sound good but if this was true, it would mean Jesus died for Gentiles only. The bible says otherwise. I memorized John 3:16 as a child and it says "whoever" believes.

For God so loved the world that he gave his one and only Son, that whoever believes in him shall not perish but have eternal life. (John 3:16 NIV)

He came to that which was his own, but his own did not receive him. (John 1:11 NIV)

The Lord told the Jewish people that He was giving a New Covenant. It was for them!

This cup is the new covenant in my blood, which is poured out for you. (Luke 22: 20NIV)

"The days are coming," declares the Lord, "when I will make a new covenant with the people of Israel and with the people of Judah. It will not be like the covenant I made with their ancestors when I took them by the hand to lead them out of Egypt, because they broke my covenant, though I was a husband to them, " declares the Lord. "This is the covenant I will make with the people of Israel after that time," declares the Lord. "I will put my law in their minds and write it on their hearts. I will be their God, and they will be my people. (Jeremiah 31:31-33 NIV)

Currently people still believe and practice that Jews can be saved apart from faith in Christ. They may not claim Dual Covenant theology but their actions prove otherwise. They believe that the Jews' faith is sufficient for salvation for them. Therefore they do not witness to Jews.

I am not ashamed of the gospel, because it is the power of God for the salvation of everyone who believes: first for the Jew, then for the Gentile. (Romans 1:16 NIV)

Paul practiced that. He preached mainly to Gentiles but he went first to the synagogue and to his own Jewish people. He believed the Messiah was the only way to salvation.

Jesus answered, "I am the way and the truth and the life. No one comes to the Father except through me. (John 14:6 NIV)

Again, salvation is the same in the New Testament as the Old Testament: By grace through faith.

It seems to me that Dual Covenant Theology is just another clever, good sounding, but evil work of Satan. His hatred of the Jewish people knows no bounds. Believers must be good students of the Bible to avoid this dangerous theology. We must check our actions with our beliefs.

Those following this Satanic theology may even love the Jews and send financial help to Israel. But they are loving them into hell. As the ministry One For Israel says, "Don't love the Jewish people more than you love the Jewish Messiah!"

The biblical command is to witness to the Jews first!

Witnessing to the Jews

As a result of the Gentiles arrogance toward the Jews, Jewish evangelism virtually stopped by the fourth century. The Gentiles had become "takers over" rather than "partakers of the promise in Christ Jesus through the Gospel." Ephesians 3:6. (Fruchtenbaum, *The Church and the Jews*, page 8)

I am not ashamed of the gospel, because it is the power of God for the salvation of everyone who believes: first for the Jew, then for the Gentile. (Romans 1:16 NIV)

What does that mean? I've learned through Dr. Arnold Fruchtenbaum's writing that the first choice is to take it literally. "If the plain sense makes sense, look for no other sense or you will end up with nonsense."

Well, I'm to witness first to the Jews! Yes, that is what Paul did even though he was the Apostle to the Gentiles. I now have a desire to witness to the Jews. I have had a few opportunities since I am now more aware of who they are and am more knowledgeable about their position in God's eye. I now look for Jews wherever I go.

Through my mentor, Miss Ruth. I have met many Jewish believers. It has been a privilege and a delight. If you need a spiritual lift, consider listening to a Jewish believer's testimony! I have also read many written testimonies. There is usually a bit of humor added to their stories. You'll come away more in awe of God and His grace.

Recently, my husband and I were invited to a fund raising banquet for a ministry out of Israel. One For Israel ministry was founded by believing Jewish men in Israel and their slogan says it all. "The best way to bless Israel is with Jesus." Their witness goes out in different ways through the internet. They understand and use the technology to connect with Israelis who are searching. They even report a revival in Israel!

As Christians we read that we are to bless Israel and many of us want to do it. We often wonder how we can do that. If you know a Jewish person, share the gospel. If you don't know any, you can support those organizations that do witness to the Jewish people. Not all organizations that support Israel witness to the Jews so check to see the ministry's actions. Pray and ask God to guide you.

One For Israel has done a great job producing videos of Jewish believers telling their story of coming to believe that Jesus is the Messiah. You can view them through their website or on Facebook. www.oneforIsrael.org Chosen People ministry also hosts a website. www.ImetMessiah.com These short videos are a real faith-lift.

History shows that most Jewish people came to faith because a Gentile believer shared the gospel with them. They became jealous and scripture commands us to make them jealous. Romans 10:19.

Let's review the elements so we are clear of what the gospel is:

- Yeshua (Jesus) died for our sins,
- He was buried,
- He rose again on the 3rd day.

It is necessary to have a willingness to believe in Yeshua as our substitute for our sins. This is explained in Fruchtenbuam, *Jews, Gentiles, Christians*, page 8.

The following scriptures will help you prepare to witness:

Romans 1:19 By faith

Romans 3:9 Jews and Gentiles alike and under sin

Romans 10:19, Deut. 32:21 Provoke to jealousy

Romans 11:11-12, 16-21 Olive tree

Acts 15:8-11 Gentiles and Jews same way to salvation

Acts 28: 25-31 Jews eyes blinded

John 12:37-43 Blinded yet many believed

Isaiah 40:1-2 Comfort, comfort my people, says your God. Speak tenderly to Jerusalem.

We can speak with kindness towards our Jewish friends. We can explain that our church doctrines came from Judaic roots. We can show our love and respect so that they feel comfortable and not threatened. We want them to become jealous in a good way of wanting to have what we have. The only way to do that is through genuine love and compassion.

I have included resources that may help you in witnessing.

Tips for Witnessing

Recently, I received a message by email from Anne Graham Lotz' ministry. If you witness to Jews, be warned that you may be criticized as she was. We need to know our scripture to refute the criticism.

Anne Graham Lotz writes:

"And this Gospel of the kingdom will be preached in the whole world as a testimony to all nations, and then the end will come" (Matt. 24:14).

What do you believe? This past week, while waiting in a car line to pick up my granddaughters at school, I heard a song on the radio that was described as the number-one Christian song in the world. It was sung by the Newsboys, entitled "We Believe."

The same week I heard the Newsboys' hit song, I read an op-ed that appeared in *The Jerusalem Post* criticizing my 911 video invitation to pray for Jerusalem because in it I implied that Jews need to be saved. Do they? Or are they exempt from the gospel?

And what is the gospel?

When the apostle Paul shared with deep conviction in Romans 1:16 that, "I am not ashamed of the gospel, because it is the power of God for the salvation of everyone who believes: first for the Jew, then for the Gentile," what was he talking about?

Prompted by the hit song and the op-ed, I have reflected on what Paul was talking about and what I believe. These are my reflections:

Everyone born into the human race is born with a sin nature, so that all are sinners.

The consequence of sin is not only physical death, but spiritual death—separation from God now and in eternity.

But God so loved the entire world of humanity that He sent His own Son, Jesus, into the world to die as an atoning sacrifice for our sin, so that whoever believes in Him will not perish separated from God, but will have eternal life.

When we confess that we are sinners, ask God to apply the death of Jesus to our sin and forgive us, He will.

Following the crucifixion of Jesus, God raised Him from the dead to give us new life here and life in heaven when we die.

When we respond and receive Jesus by faith into our hearts, He comes into us in the person of His Spirit, so that we are born again as a child of God, forgiven of our sin, and have eternal life.

When we receive Jesus Christ by faith as our Savior and Lord, we pass from darkness to light, from the power of Satan to God, from death to life.

And the gospel is this...

"Jesus said, I am the way and the truth and the life. No one comes to the Father

except through me."

"Salvation is found in no one else, for there is no other name under heaven given to men by which we must be saved." Just the name of Jesus.

"If you confess with your mouth, 'Jesus is Lord,' and believe in your heart that God raised him from the dead, you will be saved. For it is with your heart that you believe and are justified, and it is with your mouth that you confess and are saved."

"There is no difference between Jew and Gentile—the same Lord is Lord of all..."

So ... do Jews need to be saved? Yes, they do. According to God's Word, their religion does not exempt them from being sinners. Like the rest of us, they too need a Savior. Which is why God has given Jesus to be the Savior of the world.

That's the gospel that Paul was talking about. And that's the gospel I believe.

Anne Graham Lotz *is the founder of AnGeL Ministries. She is also the author of several books.*

There are many websites with help on witnessing to Jews. I have copied the following from Jews For Jesus:

Pointers on Witnessing to Jews

(from Jews for Jesus by David Brickner www.jewsforjesus.org)

Details *Category: Witnessing Last Updated on July 21, 2011 Published on July 21, 2011*
Download a printable PDF version.

Introduction

If you're reading this page, you're probably interested in sharing your faith in Y'shua (Jesus) with Jewish people! Maybe you have a Jewish neighbor…or friend, or classmate, or even a Jewish relative. Or maybe you just want to be prepared for the next time you meet a Jewish person. Here are some things you should know that will help you be a more effective witness.

Basics

Everybody needs to hear the gospel. And God's chosen people (the Jews) are certainly no exception. Y'shua came in fulfillment of the writings of Jewish prophets who were writing to Jewish people. So, if Jews don't need Jesus, no one does! Yes, Jews and Gentiles both need salvation in Jesus and you don't have to be Jewish to have an effective witness to Jewish people.

Jewish Identity and Belief

Virtually all Jews are proud of their identity as Jews, but this does not in itself make a statement about what they believe about God. Even religious Jews may have varying beliefs about God. It is more important to find out what your friend believes about God and the Bible than to find out what kind of synagogue they attend. For many Jews, their Jewish identity is more cultural than it is religious. But this doesn't mean that their Jewishness is unimportant to them. Most Jews also think that the opposite of Jewish is Christian and so for them to consider Jesus is problematic because it means considering losing their Jewish identity. Therefore in witnessing to Jewish people about Jesus it is important to stress that they do not need to give up their identity as Jews in order to embrace Jesus as Messiah.

Myths and Facts

There are several popular myths which keep people from sharing with their Jewish friends. Some of them include:

Myth: All Jews are well versed in the Old Testament. **Fact:** Most Jews have a strong cultural identity with a very limited knowledge of the Scriptures.

Myth: I can just invite my Jewish friend to my church. **Fact:** Many Jewish people might be hesitant to attend church. There is no substitute for you personally sharing your faith.

Myth: I may not be able to answer their questions. **Fact:** That's true. But it does not change the truth of the gospel. Tell your friend you are happy to research the information. This gives you an opportunity to have further witnessing opportunities too.

Myth: I need to wait for the Holy Spirit's leading. I don't want to lose my friendship. **Fact:** God has already told us we are to be his witnesses. (Mt.28:19-20) If you are friendly and forthright you will gain your friends respect for genuinely caring even if they don't agree to discuss the matter at length.

Myth: I will let my life be a testimony and wait until they ask me about Jesus. **Fact:** That will likely be a long wait. Most Jewish people feel that religion is a private matter and might be uncomfortable asking. Besides, the great commission commands us to go tell!

Practical Tips

When witnessing to a Jewish person, remember:

Make friends. Demonstrate that you really care about the person. Affirm the fact that you know they are Jewish and that you appreciate their Jewishness. Let your friendship serve as the foundation for your witness to them.

Be up front. Declare yourself a follower of Jesus right away. You do not want to appear deceptive or coercive. Be yourself.

Ask questions. Everyone likes to be asked their opinion. This can be a good way to steer the conversation towards spiritual matters. Questions about Israel, an upcoming Jewish holiday or even a Bible question from the Old Testament are a good place to start.

Give a personal testimony. The reality of God in your life is a powerful witness. Many Jewish people think that you were born a Christian in the same way that they were born Jewish. Hearing how you became a follower of Jesus, how God answers your prayers can provoke your Jewish friend to jealousy. (Rom.11:11)

Use Scripture. Don't be afraid to answer questions with a verse from the Bible. Encourage your Jewish friend to read the New Testament. Most Jewish people have never read the New Testament and most Jews who have come to faith in Christ came as a result of reading the New Testament. After all, it is a very Jewish book!

Be prayerfully persistent. Don't be put off if you receive a negative reaction at first. In Fact, you should expect it. Keep looking for opportunities. Keep praying. Seek to introduce your friend to a Jewish believer or to one of us in Jews for Jesus. Lend books or other evangelistic literature.

Ask for a decision and follow up. Don't think that your Jewish friend will automatically understand they need to pray to receive Christ. If they are a willing listener then you should ask if they are willing to receive what you have said for themselves. Be diligent to follow up any decision. Contact Jews for Jesus for help with the new Jewish believer.

Number of Jews

Today Jews are only two-tenths of a percent of the world population. Remember six million died during the Holocaust. How many Jews would there be if there had not been the enemies killing them? Demographers estimate that there should be 500 million Jews alive in the world today. (Reagan, Lamplighter, March-April, 2015)

Believing Jews, Messianics in Israel, were estimated at 5,000-6,000 in 1999 and by 2009 grew to about 15,000. Messianic ministry One For Israel reports those numbers are growing in Israel.

About 80% of the Christian believers in Israel are Arab. They are also the descendants of Abraham like the Jews but they can never be classed as Jews. One For Israel has a school with bible studies where the believing Arabs and Jews study together!

In 1900 there were about forty thousand Jews in Israel. Today there are more than six million. Netanyahu has called recently for more to immigrate. This is a modern day miracle confirming prophetic scriptures of the regathering of the Jews in the End Times.

Taking the time to study prophecy will increase your faith. It will inform you of the importance of Israel and the Jews to God. The bible refers to God as "The Holy One of Israel" and "The God of Israel." David Reagan has written many books about prophecy that are easy to read and understand. Ignorance of prophecy is to our detriment.

Chief Joy

I picked up the phone in our hotel room in Jerusalem and I heard a man with a Dutch accent asking for me by name. It was 2007 and before the trip I had emailed this man who had a ministry in Israel. Our connection was that he knew Corrie. He said he would come to the hotel and meet with me for a few minutes. I was exhausted from touring all day but I sprang into action to get to the lobby and hear more about Corrie!

Jan Willem Van der Hoeven was a young man in 1945. His family lived down the block from the Ten Boom home. His father opened their (larger) home for Corrie to come and have groups to hear about her experience during the occupation of Holland and in the Concentration Camp. He said, "At that time, you could still hear the Nazi boot heels pounding the streets."

Mr. Van der Hoeven told me that hearing Corrie's story was life-changing for him. His love of the Jewish people grew. He later moved to Israel and began his ministry there in Jerusalem.

I told him my story of loving Corrie and then starting my ministry. I explained, "I am looking for ways to expand my ministry." He quickly responded with "Make Jerusalem your chief joy and God will expand your ministry."

With those words this Dutch man, busy with his ministry to the Jewish people and teaching Gentiles to love Israel, quickly left me to ponder his words. I loved Israel but was there more to it? I didn't know what to do with that piece of advice but I never forgot it. I later marked the passage in my bible.

…if I do not consider Jerusalem my highest joy. (Ps. 136:6b NIV)

In 2016 I attended the Lamb and Lion Prophecy Conference and I had a table for my ministry. Since starting my Loving Israel 101 seminar I like decorating my table with an Israeli flag and some Judaica I've collected. I had my books The Weaving: a Journey to Corrie ten Boom Live and My Son, My Son on the table. At each end I decorated with Loving Israel cards to advertise the seminar. Of course, those were free so I passed out dozens of those. I also told those from out of town that I'd love to bring the seminar to their town. People can tell that I am passionate about this subject!

Early the following Monday morning I prayed through my prayer list first. I always pray for my ministry but this morning I had reminded myself, and the Lord, that it was His ministry, not mine. My bible passages that morning included a passage in Isaiah.

Then you will call , and the Lord will answer; you will cry for help, and he will say: Here am I.(Is. 58:9NIV)

Within a few minutes the phone rang and I picked it up. It was a man from out of town that I had spoken with at the conference. He wanted to come to my seminar and bring his friends! And he wanted to bring me and the seminar to his town!

I got off the phone and had a sweet time with my Lord, the Holy One of Israel. I had tears of joy. It doesn't get better than that.

Later as I was recounting this to my husband, I remembered, "Make Jerusalem your chief joy." I realized the Lord had been working that out in me for a very long time. All praise and glory to the God of Israel! Loving Israel yields many blessings.

Blessings for our Love

Remember that the Abrahamic Covenant holds the framework for the bible. Abraham was promised that all the peoples of the earth would be blessed through him. It did not depend on anything he did. How are Gentiles blessed by the Jews?

We have received:

- The Scriptures
- The Savior
- Salvation
- The Concept of the Local Church
- Spiritual Blessings (Fruchtenbaum, *The Book of Romans and The Jews, The Church and the Jews.*)

They were pleased to do it, and indeed they owe it to them. For if the Gentiles have shared in the Jews' spiritual blessings, they owe it to the Jews to share with them their material blessings. (Romans 15:27 NIV)

We are debtors to the Jews! That fact should be the basis for our attitude to the Jewish people.

Let's look at the statement of Dr. Mitch Glaser, head of Chosen People ministry:

"God created the Jewish people to be a blessing to the world, to be a holy people, Kingdom of Priests and a witness of the one true God. Israel was chosen and called to reveal the glory of God to the nations of the world and ultimately to lead the world to the Messiah....It may be said, based upon the Abraham covenant that God created and chose the Jewish people for the sake of the Gentiles. The penultimate purpose of God for the Jewish people was to use His chosen nation as His instruments in turning the nations to the God of Israel through the Messiah Jesus."

Dr. Mitch Glaser, The People, The Land, and The Future of Israel, page 275

My mentor, Corrie ten Boom expressed her experience:

Corrie ten Boom, Messages of God's Abundance, page 101-102

"So many Christians prayed and fasted during the Six Day War in Israel in 1967. I believe in the blessing of Abraham for people and nations: "I will bless those who bless you and, and whoever curses you I will curse" (Gen. 12:3). Nations are also being blessed; the peoples who are prepared to stand up for the Jews can expect a blessing from God. That I, an eighty-year-old, may still do such wonderful work is such an unusual blessing. Very few my age are still able to work like this. I sometimes ask myself if this is the blessing given to me by the Lord because my family and I dedicated our lives to saving Jews, and four of us died...Lord, we pray for the peace of Jerusalem and the salvation of the Jews. Preserve and protect them. They are so often in such great danger. Open the eyes of Your Children for the blessing that you give them...In Jesus' name, Amen."

If we were honest we would see how much we are blessed by God's chosen people. Reading the scriptures of the Jews we learn of the sinfulness of man and the grace of God. As we look at history the Jews teach us to rise above circumstances. No other group has survived such opposition for so long. So few in number yet they have made huge contributions to the world in all fields of work.

I challenge you to look for the contributions of the Jews. Look at Israel and see the desert blooming and yielding food. Look at Israel's technology. You'll be amazed. Clearly the Jewish people have blessed the nations. Recognizing the blessings will spur you on to bless them.

Loving Israel

My passion is to stir up love for the Jews. We are their debtors. God loves them. We are commanded to share His love and the way of salvation to the Jew first.

Andrew Murray in his book, <u>Humility: The Beauty of Holiness</u>, says, "There is no love without humility at its root."

Love is patient, love is kind. It does not envy, it does not boast, it is not proud. It does not dishonor others, it is not self-seeking, it is not easily angered, it keeps no record of wrongs. (1 Corinthians 13:4-5 NIV)

An attitude of humility is the key. We can ask God to change our heart and make it more like His heart for His chosen people. If we love the Jewish people we will want to be with them. Find them so you can spend time with them.

The Jewish people need to see our love demonstrated by our actions rather than just talk. We can earn their trust over time with patience and a sensitivity towards them.

Miss Ruth told me to begin by agreeing with all the things you both believe. That works in any relationship. Focus on your commonalities.

Three areas to bless Israel can include:

- Witnessing, not converting, the best way to bless Israel is with Jesus
- Monetary help to Messianic groups, ministries devoted to witnessing to Jews, ministries teaching the Jewish roots of Christianity
- Praying for the peace of Jerusalem, Jewish people, the land of Israel, the return of the Messiah

Pray for the peace of Jerusalem: "May those who love you be secure. May there be peace within your walls and security within your citadels." For the sake of my brothers and friends, I will say, "Peace be within you." For the sake of the house of the Lord our God, I will seek your prosperity. (Psalm 122:6-9NIV)

We also need to show solidarity with the land of Israel and the Jewish people. Join the angels to be watchmen on the wall.

I have posted watchmen on your wall, O Jerusalem (Isaiah 62: 6 NIV)

Vote on the basis of where the candidate stands on Israel. Visit the land of Israel. You'll never be the same.

One of my favorite verses from Proverbs:

"What is desired in a man is kindness." (Prov. 19:22a NKJ)

Not intelligence or money or status but kindness. The world needs kindness. Israel and the Jewish people especially need kindness.

*Comfort, comfort my people, says your God. Speak tenderly to Jerusalem …*Is. 40:1 NIV

I have heard love described as like a prism. As the light of the Jewish Messiah shines through us to His chosen people, the colors are endless. The ways to love and bless Israel are endless. Be available to shine that light. Pray earnestly for opportunities.

You are not here by accident, you are reading because you want to learn. God knows. God has promised blessings for blessing Israel. There is a joy in obedience. I pray that you will experience the joy of loving Israel: God's chosen people and the land promised to them. As that joy grows in you, do others the favor of passing it on. God promises a blessing!

Bibliography

Reagan, David. *The Jewish People: Rejected or Beloved*. McKinney, Texas: Lamb & Lion Ministries, 2014.

Reagan, David. *Anti-Semitism: It's Roots and Perseverance*, McKinney, Texas, The Lamplighter, www.lamblion.com 2007.

Fruchtenbaum, Arnold., *Jews, Gentiles, and Christians*. San Antonio, Texas: Ariel Ministries, 2005, www.ariel.org

Fruchtenbaum, Arnold. *The Church and the Jews*. San Antonio, Texas: Ariel Ministries, 2005. www.ariel.org

Fruchtenbaum, Arnold. *The Book of Romans and the Jews*. San Antonio, Texas: Ariel Ministries, 2005. www.ariel.org

Fruchtenbaum, Arnold. *How to Destroy the Jew*. San Antonio, Texas: Ariel Ministries, 2005. www.ariel.org

Couch, Mal. *To the Jew First...* Clifton, Texas: Scofield Ministries, 2009

Ten Boom, Corrie, *Messages of God's Abundance*. Grand Rapids, Michigan, Zondervan, 2002

Bock, Darrell and Glaser, Mitch, *The People, The Land, and The Future of Israel*, Grand Rapids, MI, Kregel, 2014

Shaeffer, Edith, *Christianity is Jewish*, Wheaton, Illinois, Tyndale, 1975

Other useful websites:

www.chosenpeople.com

www.jewsforjesus.org

www.oneforIsrael.org

About The Author

Evelyn Hinds is a speaker and author. She is the founder of Arts Touching Hearts, Inc., a ministry committed to expressing the message of God through the arts. She is a spokesperson for the Corrie ten Boom House and Museum in Holland. In addition to speaking and writing, she performs a one woman show as Corrie.

Additional copies of this book as well as Evelyn's book "My Son My Son" are available at http://www.amazon.com/.

To contact Evelyn or to order her first book called "The Weaving" email her at evelyn@evelynhinds.com or call 972-401-8907.

Evelyn's website is www.evelynhinds.com.